Traces of Autumn

Jen Selinsky

Kindle Direct Publishing

ISBN 9798649811422

*Not every poem included in this book is dated in chronological order. This is not an oversight on my part. Rather, I have made changes and substitutions over the years.

-J.L.S.

You have given me so much—

Oh, so much to look forward to

Since you have entered my life.

Days and nights sinking into

Desperation, you have saved me

From despair.

Who knows how things may

Have gone if I continued

On this downward spiral?

I would rot in an early grave,

A slave to this negativity.

But, oh, love has put an end

To it all and made me realize my worth,

Thus making me complete.

5/24/04

My life, I must not live the rest

Of it in vain, lest the aftermath

Drives me insane.

I must travel to the point of which

I am most happy.

Ten, five years ago I was not at

My emotional height.

When people learned of my plight,

They will tell me to break free—

Free from the burden that settles

Into my brain.

The rest of my life free of cynicism,

Which allows me to hide my best

Qualities from the world.

5/20/04

Oh, your departure makes me sad,

Although I am glad to know of the

Promising future ahead.

Your life, may it be full and

Prosperous—you have given so

Much to the world, who should

Be giving back to you.

Hard work and dedication have

Seen you through.

May your life give you

All the promises of the world!

5/24/04

Peace in my heart, I slowly

Ascend the stairway which

Has caught my attention.

Heart pumping and strong

Legs forward, I am thrilled

At the excitement that

Promises to be mine.

All these years I have waited.

Now I can reap the rewards

Of this splendid progress.

Tremble on, oh limbs, for you

Are a part of someone who has

Pulled herself up by her bootstraps!

5/24/04

So young, so much promise,

I can hold on to my opinion

And say that you'll go far.

You have come such a long way

Since your birth.

And, in your achieved fame,

You have kept your great modesty

And positive attitude.

You should not despair because

Of the things which may not be clear

Because you still have the chance

To pull yourself up even more.

Live for the moment and take life

By the horns.

Your happiness depends on you!

*dedicated to Justin Guarini

5/24/04

Coupled.

Do you still see the whole picture

In the grand scheme of things?

I have almost done my time,

But I am not ready to make such

A hard decision.

So much pressure, and so little

Time to lose, this is the most

Special, one woman in her twenties.

I can see where this is leading to;

All this scared confusion has me

Running to the corner.

I need Organization to help me

Though this, soon.

5/24/04

Have I hidden myself to your satisfaction?

Blending in with the works, wondering

If I could possibly be anymore silent.

Did you happen to notice that painting on the wall?

Reflective of life, reflective of my being—

A fancy piece of art, or a tasteless lie.

How can I leave this for you to decide when

I know that your judgment is impaired?

Speaking of things that are not fair,

I think I should take the prize.

One with one less rib, he who spells out

Dominance pertaining to only God's first

Of human creation.

What about the second, who is proven

To work just as well?

Should she be denied all the glory (that should

Be hers) because of the differences between

The legs?

Protected, strong, and going

On to continue her work.

That will never change,

I think that it's time

You saw the light!

5/24/04

Whatever has been said has

Been replaced with such an unkind demand.

Who is left to reprimand in this dire

Time of need?

I feel these little pinpoint pressures

Burdening the outside of my skin,

Curdling all the blood therein.

These people say that they have a

Demonstration they would like me to see.

Logic has failed me!

I cannot make sense of the muffled

Screams and incoherent talk.

This is quite a shock to see my future

In shambles all because of this miscommunication.

5/24/04

Let It Stand

Through thick and thin,

Our friendship has endured

Trying times.

But strength and a deep caring

Have held us together through

The years.

These years we call our own,

These later years of our youth,

Unmistaken and brought to mind.

Through the nights we laughed,

And the nights we cried.

Others cannot mistake or

Second guess a friendship so

Deep and a power so strong.

All through the time we have managed

To get along, and that is a most

Splendid thing!

5/25/04

This is a special moment

Reserved in time

For someone so dear

And so very near.

My little angel, my precious

Gift from God, you have

Brought me so much love,

Joy, and, laughter.

My precious pearl in the oyster,

My diamond in the rough,

Sometimes your simplicity brings

Me back to my days of youth.

And I feel so blessed to have

You in my life, my little one.

*dedicated to Ashley

5/25/04

While your eyes were still closed,

I came over to you and leaned over

To whisper in your ear.

I could have sworn that you stirred,

As if you heard every word I said.

Your mind might be contemplating

What might happen—what we would

Be doing if we were awake

Conscious is our time, we could

Do it with whatever we please;

Let us have the best of it all!

5/25/04

Ah!

I am visiting the past,

And I am thanking God

That I changed my life

For the better.

I may not have the best of it now,

But it would be horrible to have

To live the nightmares of my

Parents during my youth.

5/25/04

Today, I want you to

Realize just how special

Your life must be.

Today, God wants you to know

And feel all

The love He has

For you.

Even though each year you

Lived represents one of

Your best attributes, I cannot

Continue to count your deeds

To infinity.

But my love for you measures

My appreciation,

Which is also

Traceable to the heavens.

And a part of that is

Brought back

To me because

I got to have you

In my life.

Just like destiny

Puts us together,

The perfect pair!

*dedicated to Toni Selinsky

6/29/04

(I wish you) peace on this special day,

As God turns all His sight upon all

Your good deeds—seeing their way

To heaven's light.

May all your efforts be rewarded;

Your heart can't seem to miss.

Wrapped up in sheer delight at the

Thought of this heartfelt bliss.

I may not be there in body, but my

Heart stepped in its place.

I don't need to be in physical reach

To explore you in fond embrace!

*dedicated to Marjorie Clark

6/30/04

Allow me this time to say

That I'm sorry; allow me

This time to say that I care.

When the distance seems to

Be growing wider, please

Know that it's not because

You are in my heart as my

Nearest and dearest friend.

*dedicated to Jen Bauer

7/9/04

I do not have to worry about

Shielding my heart from the pain,

As all odds go in my favor to gain.

My dreams dragged through a mire—

With the accomplishments to which

I aspire to make my life better

Than what some might have thought it

Would be.

I have made it, despite any odds that

Played against me, but I still have a

Ways to go until I reach the status of

Human ideal.

7/9/04

I feel the need, I cannot surpass

The urge anymore,

All these bells going off in my head.

Emotion, the very fact which makes me

Glad to be alive.

I want to set up to greet the coming

Of each new day and all the beautiful

People this earth has housed;

We should smile at the good fortune

Of our neighbors and recognize our

Common thread—humanity of which

We should be grateful to share.

8/13/04

Whatever happened to him—

The man that I used to know?

Time surrounding my questions

And my thoughts.

I hope that he has moved on,

Overcoming those difficult

Obstacles in his life.

He shall be someone's husband,

Someone's father, and I will be

Glad to hear of the good news.

Through parted, (we) arrive again,

As friends, and tell each other

Our life stories.

8/13/04

Fluttering eyelids—

Lead to a sky scraper

Breathing its breath and

Stretching its lean figure.

Between the grass and the clouds,

Fingertips searching for the

Stratosphere before they

Are restored to their proper

Location.

Breath fills the belly with air

Until one can see the bony

Frame shrinking.

Concrete legs, solid and

Strong go forth to meet the

Prospects and inquiries of the day.

While arms sway in the loose breeze,

The tower windows open wide.

Look to warn this giant of any

Peril that would happen to

Cause disturbance.

Nothing from which to retreat,

This large being goes about the

Numerous tasks of the day.

Approaching comfortable familiarity,

It rushes, stirring further the breeze,

To something of which it is attached.

Colored streamers floating behind,

Catching the sun.

Great doorway partially open, as it

Lets out a contented sigh.

8/13/04

The immense gladness

Going through me is nothing,

Compared to solid joys of

Which I sing.

Human voice rivaled to

The songs of other creatures;

I can attest to the fact that one

May feel the gladness.

Enough to celebrate in song

Uplifting the voices of immaculate.

Choirs to ring through heaven's

Gates to charm the divine beings

With our humble, but earthly tune.

8/13/04

Through the greater standpoint

Of the whole of my mind's functions.

Having this on, oh how it raises

My ability to think and ponder life's

Great puzzles.

I want to make sure that it's kept

In tip top condition, raise my

Exuberance regarding my health.

And how things shall keep working

For me for the duration of my time.

Knowledge, drunk like the thirst-quenching waters;

I will eventually come to drink it all up and use it as

Great fuel for my growing mind!

8/13/04

Best to flow into plain sight,

Where I can see my friends

Looking for me.

Exit excitement and cries

Of delight when we exchange

Our kind words and gestures.

It's been quite a while since (we were)

Last in each other's company.

We fell, seeking everyone's

Kindness and love.

8/13/04

When last outside I could

See the summer leaves,

Still in tact, and the flowers

Enjoy their solid bloom.

Oh, but the winds coming in;

Bring along cold tidings

And a prelude to what is

Called Indian summer.

So sadly, as all fair summers

Must come to an end, thus

Allowing the process of life

To continue.

8/13/04

Twice more today, I shall

Receive a bout of great information,

Leading me to great inspiration.

'Tis far too early in this fine day

To give up hope for what could

Give me a start to my great immortality!

8/13/04

To need a new thought.

Oh, I must use it to back up

All the information in my head,

Until nature breaks through

With a most insightful discovery.

How much assistance could

Technology provide to the

Human race?

We are supposed to feel content,

Already living in our alleged prime.

Go on, some people are not as

Easy to please as I.

Help all those poor other bodies

Seek and recover the greatest thing,

Their health.

It keeps us going and gives us the

Greatest frame of mind to wake up

At the call of each new day.

8/13/04

Please do not speak any ill;

This gentle being has brought

Such joy to a seemingly

Helpless situation.

They are content, oh so relieved.

That this being has been allowed

To live and present its happiness

To all of those who are directly

Involved.

Please hold your tongue, for even

I can show a little bit of mercy.

8/14/04

Glowing, he cannot pretend

To see any radiance which

Is not there.

Something, ever so unexplained

Attracts him in my direction.

I can see that this has been

Happening for what some would

Like to call years.

His recent interests diving into

A cesspool of raw emotion

And admiration.

Is it possible, could I honestly

Possess every good quality that

He claims to be in my favor?

Or is he so easily blinded by

This thing called love?

I suppose I cannot lack all of

These great attributes.

8/14/04

Am I her hero, born after

Such an unlikely time?

My great health, the package

In which I was delivered,

Human female.

Other than my health, I did

Not have much of a chance,

As most everything I made

Was done from my own hands.

Fallen short of construction?

No, I just needed more time,

So grateful of that I have received.

I am going to build more on it each day

So that I do not fall short of these dreams!

8/14/04

How nice, it is always great

To hear your voice, to hear it

Become more lively when I bring

It any optimistic hope.

Oh, you and your bouts of cynicism.

I suppose that I can empathize,

But a part of me hurts so much.

When I can hear the anger in your voice,

And I can feel it in my soul.

It makes me want to cry, to think

That I could have been the same.

To think that you will be like this

Without any shame, if you don't

Allow me to help you out of this all.

My dearest friend, I do not wish to see you

On such a disastrous decline.

8/14/04

Such is the sweetness of victory,

I have seen three women set

Out to what they think is their duty—

Embarking on family and matrimony.

I would like to thank myself for

Smiling down in what some would

Think (of as) my prime, free of burden.

I am glad, oh so glad for them, but

Relieved that it is not I.

My splendid hopes plan to reach

The sky and move far away from

These kinds of things.

Oh, my lips praise the indelible mark

That I shall own one day, when people

No longer look down upon me.

8/14/04

See from the free spirit,

As it leaps from its body

And dances upon every

Cloud in the sky—blue

Azure.

Omnipresent, but moved by

The wind.

No boundaries it holds, and

Every place that it calls home.

What mortal eye can witness

It in its great transparency?

None.

Oh, but they know that such

An entity as this can be present.

8/14/04

A hint of detection
As man has crossed the sea,
Fallen victim to the façade
And their hidden hostility.

8/14/04

~~~~~~

Blood flow has been stopped,
A certain possibility for the
Body to heal.
The man was in his youth
Attacked, hospitalized, and
Gauzed. The medical staff
Knows what's best to clot the bleeding,
Eyes wide.

8/14/04
~~~~~~

Understanding

The tragedy.

Oh, then, people

Could not understand

Medicine, human behavior

As it is diagnosed today.

All the sorrow that I feel;

I hope that heaven has

Made up for the damage done.

Years of torment, screaming from

This earth, as everything they

Received at birth has been

Damaged.

Ignorance likes to have them

Dwelling in dark corners while

Misery does its toll on those

Poor, unsuspecting beings.

To think that man has allowed

All this from the beginning of time

Has me wincing and questioning

Humanity's roots.

The term had to come to be somehow,

But I think its origins more recent

After all this time to repent.

Forgive, we have all come to evolve

Through human understanding.

Kindness all through us makes

The blood remain in our veins and our

Hearts, carrying out their true function.

8/16/04

Watch me work;

See an outline of my joints

And veins as they work

Underneath my skin.

Marvel at human majesty;

Our bodies have been

Constructed to allow us

To do unbelievable things.

Maintenance, I do all that I can,

Functioning parts at the completions

Of my physical entity.

Oh! The miracles of the flesh

And blood;

See them unfold as I go about

My daily tasks.

8/16/04

I am near due

To my time

For a small bout

Of relief.

See me here,

I will not

Be in this place

Tomorrow.

The many suns

During which I wake

Will show that I

Have no regret

Because I have progressed.

No longer must I struggle

Underneath mediocrity.

8/15/04

He

Keeps a cool face

And remains happy,

No matter the outcome.

Oh, he knows he's

Cherished and that

They will stand by

And support his actions—

Through the kindness of mockery

And deceit, up to the elevated status

Where they all belong.

Faithful followers hold

Tight onto his robes until

They reach their destination w/ him.

*dedicated to Justin Guarini and his

loyal fans

8/16/04

Is it normal to feel anger,

Almost bitter hatred, at my

Frustrations?

Stuck at the mercy of them,

Unleashing their hearts from the

Inside.

My mind, overburdened, I have

Taken too much already.

Oh! If only I didn't have to worry

That my mind was going to explode.

I can't take each slow, painful

Reminder.

The burning; I want to cover my eyes

And roar in pain!

These things, dripping blood from

The inside.

On the outside, white turns to red,

As people place the blame on me.

I doubt I can last through tonight

If this keeps up the same, horrible pace.

8/17/04

I have seen,

I have started

To embark upon a journey.

All my prayers, I hope

That God sees me through

Because this would revolutionize

My whole life!

Please let me keep my ability

To do these things I hold

In my heart, oh so dear.

Life, rich in meaning.

Blood, poured out with my soul,

Making me live the stuff I bleed.

I have felt my worth; it cannot

All be taken away!

8/17/04

Fear

It is making me sane.

Pain.

My poor brain does not

Always work on their level.

Eternal,

Try to find something higher;

I have come so far.

Matter of time, it is not

My enemy yet because

I have not finished with

My transformation.

8/17/04

Calm.

Now I can feel the

Tranquility.

Ease, I can find that

I will make it through

The day and live to

Tell so many tales.

Fear not, because

God has me resting

Safely in the palm of

His hand!

8/17/04

She has

Come so far

And achieved

So much

In her young life.

Who can honestly

Say that they are

Not proud of all

That she has done?

Oh, queen of success.

Dear friend, please

Tell me how it feels

From the top once

You will reach the highest point,

Where you shall be given

What you want out of life!

8/18/04

Time

May not always

Be fair, even though

It is of the essence.

I wish I could

Do something there

To help ease the pain.

Strong warrior,

Hold on, hold on!

Grain of sand from the hourglass,

Was falling.

I wish now that

You could find all

The memories—see

How great your

Life was and how

Things could be.

My heart to yours,

Sorrow, that I did

Not know you better.

Distance,

That is the

Worst thing

Holding us back

On our way

To see you—

To check your progress.

We need

More of that.

Hope, I've asked

My friends to

Help with prayer,

Which is all we

Can do right now—

Larger strength

In numbers.

We love you!

*dedicated to Daniel E. Clarke II

8/18/04

Good woman,

This is just as hard on you.

Devotion, you stay strong

To your oath.

Persistent through weather,

Like the mighty oak.

Oh! How I wish the sun

Would brighten for you

This day. Last time, it was

Hidden some by clouds.

Our sorrow, the other

Sides of our hearts go

Out to you!

Whatever happens, we need

Fortune on our side

So that we can rest assured.

That things will

Turn out all right;

We want this unnecessary toil to end.

Such a great person and a good friend,

We must condone you for your

Great actions.

Love and support, we know

That God will provide, but we give

What we can on earth as a pledge.

Of our faithful love in hopes that

Greatness will see its way through.

*dedicated to Marjorie L. Clarke

8/18/04

The sun will not forget to shine

And share its warmth for those

Who have just awakened.

Though I may not see clearly,

I can feel it in my eyes and my soul—

The strength of summer's warmth

Out to enlighten all these lives,

Who feel that they need some

Additional meaning amidst the

Variety of their days. All of this

Is for you, for the answers to all

Your questions, which comprise your lives.

8/19/04

I can still remember

The days when we

Tried to hide from you

And your annoying nature.

Cruel, but true.

There was no way of getting

Around your thoughts—

Opinions trailing behind for

All the world to see.

And the earth was supposed

To shake underneath your feet.

All of those you thought

Inferior were supposed to

Respect you,

Even though they

Had no clue. But it was really

You who wandered alone in

The dark, wondering why no one

Wanted to be seen with you.

Who could blame them?

But I could not blame you

For trying whatever it is

You wanted to prove to this world

Of people who do not understand.

Now I am glad that all is said

And done so we can finally

Go our separate ways.

8/19/04

High school friends

Have proven to be

Most true.

(Those of you I've met

In college have nearly

Faded away.)

High school friends

Have seen me through.

So much good and bad;

Their compassion remains a

Priority in my heart.

And we shall stand strong

Through the winds of

Adversity and change,

Knowing that we can

Triumph over anything!

*dedicated to Jen Bauer, Chris LoBue, and Jim Rebholz

8/20/04

Everyone agrees

That times have

Changed since then.

How much; how so?

Many of you still

Recognize me as the

Same person, but so different.

Some say that I have changed,

For better or for worse.

Someone can't make

The distinction, so I'll

Keep track of all the

Changes myself.

This way, things will work.

8/21/04

My precious summer

Is eluding me, falling

Out of my grasp and

Leaving me to the devices

Of winter.

What else have I to do

But accept the terrible direction

In which this is going?

Wishes that this would never

Come to an end, broken

And sent to the past.

It's too late; nothing I can

Do right now will change

The direction of the seasons.

8/21/04

Clenching my fist

On the glass and watching

The blood trickle down my

Fingers, I have realized my life

Has come to naught,

And my blood has already

Corrupted the earth.

I wish there was some way

I could take it all back,

But no one can recall

These atrocities.

Black, sinking in.

I will remove my stained mark

From this earth!

8/22/04

Swept ashore—

The froth against my skin.

Footsteps from the man

Who has come to take

His claim with me.

Seconds into the ways

Of the world!

He draws me in for a

First kiss.

I don't know which muscles

To tense, but he seems

To know his way around

My anatomy.

Interconnected thoughts,

This man has made me

Feel as one with him.

No longer do I fear…

8/22/04

Strong,

You have been able

To stand up through storms.

No weather can take you down,

And no one can make you

Lose your grace.

(You've seen) so much

In such a little amount of time;

I admire you for your courage

And perseverance.

These things, relating back to me.

I am glad that I have been able

To help see you through.

My friend, *mein comerade*,

You overshadow all in your

Magnificent glory.

You are a survivor and a lesson

To all who are weak!

8/22/04

You made her cry,

But we end up

Taking your side.

Things should

Work out because

Your life is just

Starting to form.

Youth have it hard.

They have to strive;

Do not discourage

Them in any way!

She has done so much

With her little life,

Only to have

Everything be

Shot down by

Your flying flack.

Torpedoes.

Desperation,

You had better

Hope that she

Does not give up

Her lifetime dreams

As she climbs higher

The ladder—to

Obtain her

Long-awaited success!

8/22/04

A smile,

I almost

Forgot myself

In the midst

Of this "old" confusion,

But I am back

To my normal state.

Second long

Snap into reality;

I am glad that

My delusion didn't

Last long.

8/22/04

You know better

Than to provoke

Someone of this nature.

You don't know what

She can do when

Her wrath is unveiled.

She holds no mercy

When her brain is

Full of anger, so

She can turn over

The world and scramble

Us all with her forefinger,

Making us go off course and

Forgetting why we are alive.

8/22/04

What ill befalls me now?

I try to give myself the nutrition

That's most essential.

Body malfunction,

This can only slow

Things down and worsen

My condition even more.

I'll not have it!

My life is far too

Important to live

Without being in

Splendid condition.

8/22/04

These lost days

Have me scrambling

For my sanity,

For the nerve that I lost;

And am going to lose.

Hard to keep the pieces

Together, adhesive

Wearing off, trying

To retrieve the glue.

I cannot fulfill my

Duties in pieces.

My life, my life

Requires stability, so

I cannot run out and

Scream into the silence,

Disturbing the peace

Of those who want to

Enjoy every fragile detail.

I must save these bouts

For the paper on which I write!

8/22/04

Can I say that I'm

Going to be relieved,

Or should I feign

Some full-frontal

Sincerity?

Oh, life does not want me

To worry about these details,

So minute

That they cannot be

Detected by the

Naked eye alone.

I have larger demons to slay,

But it's still a matter

Of surviving the next few days,

Thus telling the world that

I am durable!

8/22/04

I don't believe

In wasted time,

Or wasted space,

In this case.

Fill me up with inspiration,

And I can take you to

Different worlds.

8/22/04

So much time

For you to pull

Me apart

With your decisions.

Make up your mind!

Plotting and planning

What you will do to me,

Either way, I feel

I cannot win.

8/22/04

Until He Comes

Until he comes

To kiss my eyelids

And set me to sleep,

I lie awake and

Make sure that my

Dreams do not

Escape my head.

Until he comes,

I must try to relax,

Though I have to

Fight off any

Invaders alone.

Stuck wanting to

Exit this world

For a time, to

Leave my weary

Body behind.

Until he comes,

The tide must

Remain low,

And my profile

Will be known

As my earthly

Name alone.

No more promises

Of individuality.

After I leave,

But who really

Needs these things

When they are ready

To be replenished?

Until he comes,

My body must remain firm.

8/22/04

She is not here;

She's gone far, far away.

The greater part of me

Not stopping to care as

I move on with my life.

Things have to be done,

And she might come back

In the midst of it all.

That is the surviving thought

That helps me out the most.

8/23/04

He dreams in armies,

So safe that he can

Assume the role

And form what is

Known as a modern

Dictatorship.

Soldiers marching through

The villages and stomping

Our dreams into the ground.

Her red eyes, burning

Into our souls

And draining us of our will.

Resentment brews in our blood,

But there is nothing we can do

Because this plague has already

Come to eliminate us all.

8/23/04

Stirring up some

Controversy; people

And their mixed feelings

Have a way of trying to

Make others see their

Ways as the only life.

That can only lead

To nowhere fast, all

The years have said.

8/24/04

I want it back!

Let me have it back.

Days, months ago,

Years coming back

Into my life, making

Me relive the horror

That made my

Self-worth practicality

Nonexistent.

Depression sinking in

As the food sticks

To my body and hides

My current identity.

To come out, making

Enough to hover over

To my destination.

8/24/04

You remind me of

Someone from the past,

Someone who drifted in

And out of my life so fast.

I wonder where you are now

And what you have done

For the last few years.

Vague, I wonder what started

This recollection—such a

Minute part of my mind; this

May never come again until these

Words bring themselves into

My head.

8/24/04

Leave the man alone,

Can't you see that he

Is trying his best to

Do what he can?

Unclear, people may

Not always pay

Attention to the words—

Too busy in their criticism.

Ah! The curiosity has

Gotten to our brains

And made them believe that

These harsh words are right.

No one should have

To endure this kind of pain,

Especially one who is

Trying to make his mark

On the world.

8/24/04

I Tried

I tried,

Lord, I have tried

To do these things.

To give my body rest;

God knows that I

Cannot live on

Consciousness alone.

Immortality, I

Achieve that at night,

When my body is

Separated from my mind.

I miss that,

How I need

It right now.

I tried to

Get something

My body requires,

But I failed.

Now I must pay

The price until

I can close

My eyes again.

8/24/04

You don't know

How happy he can

Make me; you

Can't possibly

Know how his loving

Embrace soothes me,

As he runs

His fingers

Through my hair and

Whispers in my ear.

One cannot

Fathom how

Much he moves my world

When he speaks of my

Beauty in such a way

That it will always be

Admired.

Things brought on

By this condition,

Which can only be

Considered love in

Its unconditional

Meaning.

It has happened

So strong

This time because it has

Redefined my world.

8/24/04

Strutting

In the rain—

Something that

I usually do not do,

But I have to explore

Other possibilities.

Wet droplets

Cling to my skin,

Is this for my benefit

Or theirs?

Slicked back hair and

Garments soaked, who

Can see me now?

It was all their idea

At first, I find that I

Enjoy this kind of thing,

So organic.

I guess it can do

Wonders for my skin.

8/24/04

I can only hope

That they do not

See me here,

Dressed in my poorest

And standing on

My lowest point.

Some people have been

Questioning my existence

For quite some time.

That is all right, let

Their minds think

Of the endless possibilities,

That is, if they are wrong

About my current situation.

8/24/04

When the sunlight

Burns stronger in my eyes,

It reminds me that summer

Is coming to an end.

Alas! I must experience

The same thing every year.

Circulating depression,

It is essential, even though

It doesn't have to be.

Only my mind can

Control how I feel.

8/24/04

This is an outrage!
Pluck me bald, and
Strip me blind, then
Spit upon my rights as
A human being.
You make me beg, you
Make me gravel for
The things that the
Common man deserves.
Too late, my nose has
Already been stuck
In the air.
Too late to watch me
Roll up my sleeves
And spit on my hands.
No!
You've held back
Long enough for me
To have lost any dignity,
So no one can expect me to
Go back in the right direction.
Watch me bite, sweat, kick

And bleed just to raise

Myself to the next level,

When I can finally walk

Erect and greet the world

As a real human being.

8/24/04

We'll see what we can

Do about today, but tomorrow

Is still another story, unhinged.

Take it one day at a time;

That's the way to go!

8/24/04

Once Ago

Once ago,

I was young.

What memories my

Poor mind can hold

Are enough to last me

A lifetime once the final

Flavor of my youth is

Completely gone.

Ashamed, no, I have

Already come to

Accept it,

Sometimes.

Let it go, let it go.

Everyone has to

Eventually

Let this go.

Once ago, I was known

For my exuberant struggles,

But time has to resist

These things

That used to excite me.

The wild ideas

Of my body have left me,

So I find myself in a humble

Old state.

8/24/04

Gone too fast;

It was never meant

To last.

Whirlwind romance,

Dashed up against

The rocks!

8/24/04

Quite comical,

As the eyes of

The young men pay

Their undying attention

To the scantily clad women

Playing volleyball on the beach.

One is wounded—shoulder bandage.

Watch the flexing muscle

In the organic struggle of the flesh.

I want to move like them,

While the lonely man in the booth

Would like to be with one of them,

Or maybe all of them.

I can see me with such a great physique,

Statuesque and admired by many.

8/24/04

Ah! Sweet coincidence

He is here, by my side.

Loved ones close by

In the distance, I can

See their focused smiles

As they send a friendly

Wave in my direction.

The epitome of irony

And joy of my day;

I'm so happy to know

That I can spread my mirth

To others!

'Tis such a gift!

8/24/04

So many farewells;

People come into my life

And go out like a flame.

Wondering if we ever will

Meet again under

Coincidental circumstances

And exchange brief conversations.

Strange how some things work

Out this way.

8/24/04

Oh!

He has done

It again;

Mentioned the word,

Planted the seed

In my head.

Rather, he has tried

But, thus far, he has

Had many

Unsuccessful

Attempts.

Words to

Scare this

Human being,

Shaking

And threatening to

Change the position

Of my soul.

Jitters, more than

A mild case.

Soon it will cause

My breath to

Come to a halt.

We don't want that,

Especially if his

Intentions

Want to go through!

8/24/04

Watch her tongue

And lips, flapping

Around dead air

And turning it into gossip.

Restless, they want to talk

Their useless talk, but I

Do not want to listen…

…Priceless, a moment

Of silence; I know that

They are avoiding me,

But I do not care!

It has no meaning to me.

8/24/04

Fragranced,

I can sense every

Part of the atmosphere

Wafting in and out

And making this place

Come alive—not that

It even takes too much

Effort.

8/24/04

If you want to make me

Nauseous, you are on the

Right track.

Forcing, pushing these

Roles into

Our heads

And into the corrupted

And uncorrupted

Minds of those I am

Trying to avoid.

Anticipation; you had

Better believe

That I want to

Leave as soon as I can,

Especially since I am so

Strange to the others.

They are pushing me

Out of the box;

Let them

Push me so that I never

Have to see them again.

It would be a blessing!

(Until then I have to

Pass the time…)

8/24/04

~~~~~~

All their tiny secrets

Will be revealed

To the world,

As soon as their

Lips leak the words

To those who are

Willing to listen.

8/24/04
~~~~~~

Do I dare question your authority,

If that is what you would like to call it?

I should only have to listen to myself

And those who matter in my life,

So what am I doing here?

I ask myself that question when

I come in contact with this place.

Looming figures threaten

My gentle presence and cries of pain

From within.

8/24/04

"Well, well, well,"
The man
Behind the desk said,
Folding and unfolding
His hands as the probable
Profits walk by.
Barren hotel, located
In a hole;
It's a dying business.
He has the manner
Of a vulture, and
Anyone that
Walks through
Those doors
Falls victim
To the predators.
They have some food
And beer to go, though
Everyone is
Tired of the
Cardboard taste.
We can relate, but we

Don't want to

Be associated

With this drunken vestibule

Who wants to take over

His small portion of the world!

8/24/04

Flash bulb photography

In black and white.

Steal a picture of the girl

And mount her on the

Back of the book.

'30s style; I don't think

They do that anymore.

You can catch me on the

Internet, color photo scanned,

Biographical detail.

Face of my ancestors,

How all the times have changed.

Living in the modern era,

You can see me now.

8/24/04

Here's hoping that life

Will give you all the best

That it has to offer;

Here's hoping that you

Will have fond memories

Of the past and bright

Dreams for the future.

Look ahead and achieve all

That you have the capacity to

Because you are spectacular.

8/24/04

What else can I say?

It has been a pleasure

Working together

And helping each other out

As much as we can.

Engaging in conversation,

Leading soon a session of

Reminiscing, we find

Out that we have things

In common, and we find

Laughter in each other's

Company.

So great to have met you!

8/24/04

Cooling Off

Counting the days,
Trying to get over
My fears before I have
To go back and face
What challenges life
Likes to give to see.
If I can keep up with
The world, I can keep up
With these things.
Cooling off is the only
Thing that makes me
Feel as if I have any
Control—start at ten
And go back to zero.
That is how the process
Is done.

8/25/04

Loud,
What you hear
Coming from the
Inside of my soul.
Fiery, mad; this
Time, you cannot
Say, "Just let it go."
You have let it go
Too many times before.
Hear me out, no
Other option.
Hear me out, some things
Have already been said.
Nothing can quench
The flame until all
The bitterness has
Been expressed.

8/25/04

A modern love tragedy,

These two were never

Meant to be, even though

They sent off so much

Electricity.

Cheers, hopes, and prayers,

I wanted to have things

Otherwise.

In the cards, all the cards;

They had to go their

Separate ways.

A great mismatch, trying to

Survive every storm so

They can frolic in the

Spring meadow.

It may happen again, but

It will not last for long.

Nothing does in this world,

Their world of insecurity.

8/25/04

Reversal roles,

He tries to instill

Some kind of sick point.

I suppose that he is right,

But he should have

No power under these

Circumstances.

Crime does not pay;

Crime does not comprise

The good aspects of

Humanity!

What was I thinking?

No one should have

These bad things on

Their minds to lead

To the corruption of

Human kind.

Reverse the aforementioned

Events (to make amends).

8/25/04

Someone clapped

Behind me.

The echo from the

Distance caused me

To turn my head.

Who was trying to

Get my attention;

Who wanted to see me

So desperately?

It seems as though

Years have passed since

People have requested my

Company.

Eye-blinking confusion,

I know not what was

Going on, but I have

The feeling that things

Are going to change.

8/25/04

You like to have me;

You like practically

Every move that I make.

Undying devotion,

You have pledged

This to me.

Sometimes,

I do not understand why

He has picked me; I

Suppose that a good

Part of me has

Touched his fancy,

Swept him away to

A land which may not

Have been seen by

Him before.

I just hope that he

Finds all that he

Wants from what I

Have to offer.

8/25/04

Exchanging stories between

Two lovers at different times.

Neither one understood the other

Cruel words exchanged—less

Than kind thoughts.

They would hate each other

Right now and spit in one

Another's face.

Aye! They both had their

Way with me.

Past and present struts, one hidden,

Now seen—growling at the

Offenders who have tried to go

Too far right before drawing me back

Into their arms.

Something in common, protective nature,

Inherent in many life forms.

8/25/04

Thank God for you!
All great things you
Have said and done.
You've helped me up
From the ditches and
Made me realize that
I can soar!
Once shielded by my hands,
You helped me open my eyes.
After failure, after humiliation
Helped me force myself out.
When all I wanted to do
Was hide from the world,
You made me realize that none
Of my dreams were insignificant,
As long as I did my best to
Pursue them.
My biggest fans, always
Encouraging me to do what
I do best.
Nothing more and nothing less,
And I hope that I have stood

By you as you have stood by me.

And I wish to thank you

For all the undying love

You've given me over the years;

It means so much!

*dedicated to all my friends and family

8/25/04

Extended outward,

I appreciate him

Extending his hand

Out toward mine.

I never thought

That it would happen,

But my time has

Finally come.

Yes, I am going to feel

Almost first-hand.

For the first time,

Something seems so real!

8/25/04

Time has seen itself

Give and take.

But time, as we know it,

Will all be changed once

We exit the formalities

Of this life.

Do you realize; I don't

Think that many people

Know what will happen to

The ethereal beings.

Souls will change, and they

Will have to get rid of

The things they valued

On earth, but it will

All be worth it once we

Know what's going on…

8/25/04

Please listen to me,

Even if you have

Something you want to say.

This will not take long

If you are willing to obey.

Do not be unkind;

Just open up your mind

And free yourself from

The words that got to you

Before mine.

8/25/04

Not giving up hope;

I am going to take

This all the way!

All the way to what is

Promised to me after

The foundation is laid.

Yes, these things will

Be displayed for so many

Eyes to read, minds to

Experience, and souls

To feel!

Let's make a deal so I can

Establish the foundation

For my immortality.

Support from friends and

Family have enabled me

To make it this far!

8/25/04

Oh! To return to sixteen in

Such an age where technology

Reigns, and the youth are not

So impressionable.

Smart minds, even though

They act like their counterparts

From twenty years ago!

Young love, radical love, and

There I was in the front,

Listening to as much of the

Conversation I could.

'Stern Papa' driving and egging them on.

O', this 'Athena' lives so close to me;

I can see that I like her already.

But jealousy rears its common head

When I feel like 'ignorant Mama'

In the front seat, trying to relate

To Papa and his progeny.

Two brothers in the same house

And this wonderful girl who is so close,

Yet so far.

She has made me feel that it's worth

It to study the love lives of these youth.

Not a thing here is being wasted, except

For my brain when it does not speak;

I tried to keep up with the conversation

Without burying myself too deep.

Long ways, here and there, with his

Hands on my back and on my knee,

Oftentimes

Smiling gently.

Two of them silent in the

Back seat of the car,

Which makes me want

To explore, again,

The fervor of my youth.

Such zeal, even these youngsters have the

Same chemistry.

Papa then looks at me and makes me

Blush inside myself, making me feel

Like the innocent schoolgirl that I never was

(Or ended up to be).

Please don't make me feel like I strove

And came up too short.

My brains, all *spectaculaire*, everything

Depends on me nipping the problem

In the bud!

8/26/04

I feel like a young knight,

On a quest to discover a

New world—to achieve

Something so high, something

That I cannot yet explain.

Such an inspiration, but so

Vexing at the same time.

It's so difficult until I can

Climb up to the window and

Receive a fair kiss from the muse

(On the forehead); then everything

Transforms

Into its medieval setting,

So illuminating!

Please don't make me mount

My horse and leave.

8/27/04

Church Mouse

How can you possibly say
That I do not keep quiet;
I need to be quiet all the time?
When things sound as if they
Shatter or break; you say I
Sound like a bull
Crashing though a china shop.
I do not mean to, I guess
It's all just innate.
But now that my poor body
Feels heavy from my tired
Muscles needing sleep, I will
Play the part of a tiny mouse,
Who will not be seen until long after
The rising of the sun.

8/27/04

Do not think that I could,

That I would forget you.

Oh, he who has given so much

Joy to those who happen

To be listening for a

Worthy cause.

Give this man some appreciation

And, in turn, make him receive

All the happiness he deserves.

Ever marching to the line

Marked *Victory*; I know so

Many are glad to help him along

As they pave the road which

Will one day lead to a stop, right

Before his greatest treasures.

8/28/04

About the Author

Jen Selinsky was born in 1978 in Pittsburgh, PA. She was raised in Cranberry Township. In December 2004, Jen earned her MLS from Clarion University of Pennsylvania. She now lives in Sellersburg, IN.

Some of Jen's short works have been published in several anthologies, including *The Raider Review*, *Tobeco*, and *Essence of a Dream*, published by The National Library of Poetry—for which her poem, "Ode to the Forest," won an editor's choice award. One of her works was also recently published in *The Poetry Review.com*.

9 798649 811422